Weird Rome: A Collection of Mysterious Stories, Odd Anecdotes, and Strange Superstitions from the Ancient Romans

By Charles River Editors

Marie-Lan Nguyen's picture of a bust of Roman Emperor Claudius

About Charles River Editors

Charles River Editors provides superior editing and original writing services across the digital publishing industry, with the expertise to create digital content for publishers across a vast range of subject matter. In addition to providing original digital content for third party publishers, we also republish civilization's greatest literary works, bringing them to new generations of readers via ebooks.

Sign up here to receive updates about free books as we publish them, and visit Our Kindle Author Page to browse today's free promotions and our most recently published Kindle titles.

About the Author

Sean McLachlan spent many years working as an

archaeologist in Europe, the Middle East, and the United States. Now a full-time writer, he's the author of many history books and novels, including *A Fine Likeness*, a Civil War novel with a touch of the paranormal. Feel free to visit him on his Amazon page and blog.

Introduction

The statue of Augustus on *Via dei Fori Imperiali* in Rome

"Rome was a poem pressed into service as a city." In that short line, Anatole Broyard, a 20th century American writer, compactly captures the timeless and enchanting beauty that resides within the Eternal City of Rome. This tourist destination is often one of the highest ranked on bucket lists, for how could one not want to experience its marvelous ruins, mirror-like rivers, and spectacular stretches of aqueducts firsthand? As one sips on fine Italian wine on a terrace overlooking the grand remnants of the Colosseum, one can practically hear the roars of the battling gladiators and the raucous applause of the spectators. And as one strolls through the coarse, yet quaint cobblestone streets, one can almost hear the galloping horses and screeching wheels of chariots in the distance, and even feel the brush of the breeze as they charge past. It is difficult not to fall in love with a city so effortlessly nostalgic it verges on utopian.

The ambitious and fearless emperors who built the legendary Roman Empire from scratch, the broad-shouldered and bronzed gladiators with their iconic plume helmets and glinting swords, and elaborate parties attended by toga-wearing Romans fueled by alcohol, violence, orgies, and other godless acts all paint a picture of Roman life. Indeed, many people are well-versed with these unique scenes of Roman history, but few are familiar with the equally riveting years preceding the dawn of the Roman Republic, and even less people are acquainted with the fabled Seven Hills sitting east of the Tiber River – the core geographical components of Rome, and the very foundations that the Eternal City was built on.

Ancient Rome is understandably an object of enduring fascination, and its legacy still survives today, especially in the West, where Roman architecture, law, and philosophy all influence modern societies. But the Romans were also startlingly different - a deeply superstitious society, they believed in all sorts of omens and magic spells, while their leaders were capable of cruelties that would make a modern war criminal blush. Regular Romans performed strange religious practices, and they engaged in even stranger sexual practices.

Weird Rome: A Collection of Mysterious Stories, Odd Anecdotes, and Strange Superstitions from the Ancient Romans looks at the more bizarre sides of Roman civilization, helping people understand the true nature of Rome and examining aspects that documentaries and museum exhibitions tend to gloss over. Along with pictures depicting important people, places, and events, you will learn about the weirder parts of Rome like never before.

Weird Rome: A Collection of Mysterious Stories, Odd Anecdotes, and Strange Superstitions from the Ancient Romans

About Charles River Editors

About the Author

Introduction

A Mystical Founding

Unusual Medical Practices

Odd Eating Habits

Strange Religious and Magical Practices

Abuses of Power

Sex and Rome

An Enduring Archaeological Mystery

Online Resources

Further Reading

Free Books by Charles River Editors

Discounted Books by Charles River Editors

A Mystical Founding

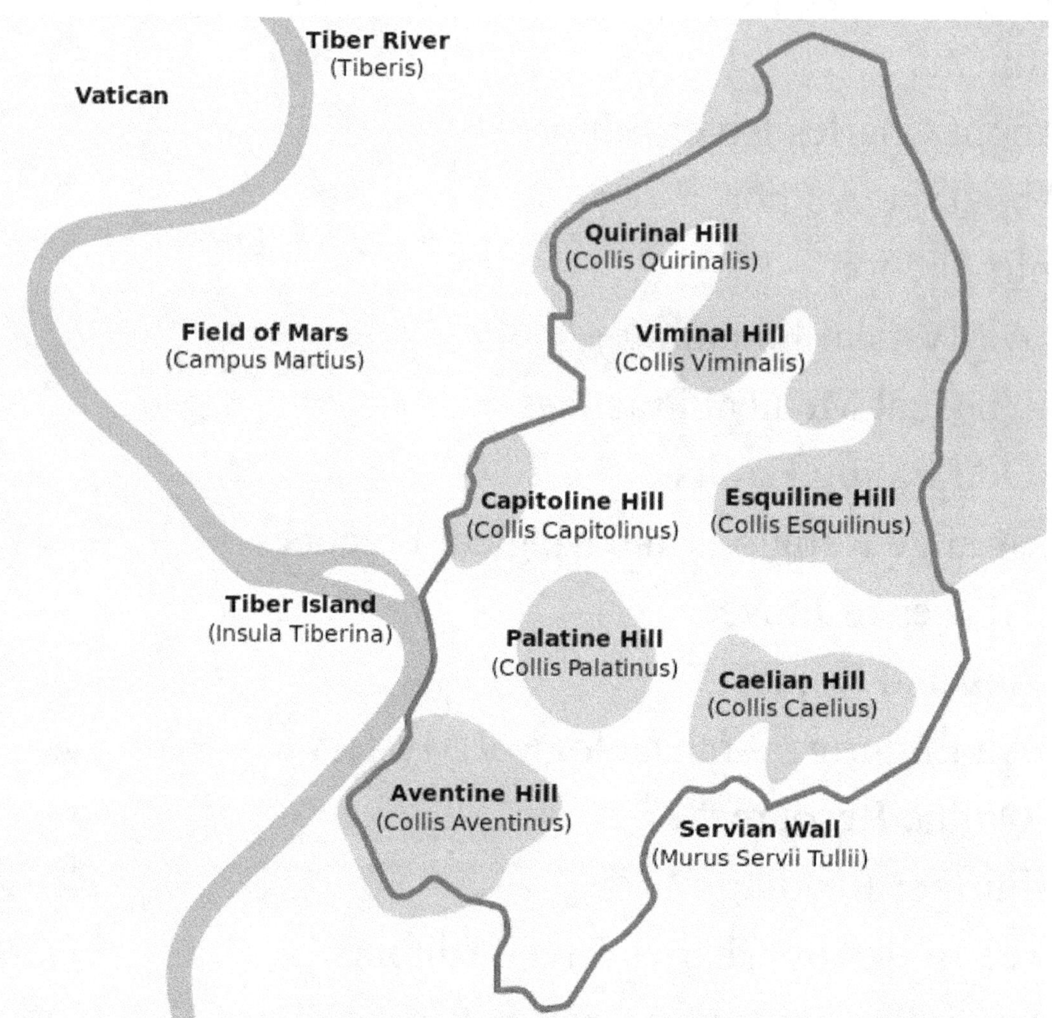

A map of the Seven Hills

"The populace like the sea is motionless in itself, but stirred by every wind, even the slightest breeze." – Livy, 1st century BCE historian

An assortment of Italic tribes had been occupying the boot of Italy long before the rise of the Romans. The bulk of these people hailed from the lands north of the Adriatic Sea, gradually moving in to the unoccupied nooks and crannies of the peninsula over the years. A fraction were Greek nomads who sailed from their motherland, docking by the shores of southern Italy. Historians described these tribes as primitive and "scarcely civilized," but these settlers, who relied mostly on their flock, would become the very first to crack into the rough earth of never-before-cultivated Italian soil. For the most part, these tribes rarely strayed from familiar territory, for conversing with one another was another struggle in itself; each spoke a crude blend of Aryan and Indo-European languages.

Four tribes composed of what is now referred to as the "Italic race" made up the majority of the population – the Latins, the Sabellians, the Oscans, and the Umbri. The Latins were predominantly in central Italy, living in villages throughout and encircling the Old Latium region, which sat between Mount Circeo and the Tiber River, as early as the late Bronze Age (1200-900 BCE). Latin villagers lived in clusters of "straw-thatched" huts, which later expanded to settlements on the Alban Hills southeast of Rome. When the city erected defensive walls in later years, many of these villages blossomed into cities, bound together by a common language and their worship for Jupiter, the supreme Roman god of light and sky.

The Sabellians, often depicted as a fierce and warmongering people, lived to the south and east of their Latin and Oscan neighbors by the Appenine Range. Since green thumbs were a rarity among the Sabellians, the villagers banked on their livestock, or the booty obtained from looting the harvests of nearby villages for sustenance.

The Oscans, who inhabited the lands southward of the Old Latium, were also quick to grab their spears. They shared many customs with the Latin tribes, but lagged a step behind when it came to agricultural methods, technological innovations, and the general advancement of their society. Many of their descendants, such as the Volscians, Aequians, and Hernicans, would later engage skirmishes with the Romans.

The Umbri were supposedly the oldest of all Italic tribes. The spelling of the original name, "*Ombrii*," which translates to the "people of the thunderstorm," was given to them by the Greeks, for the Umbri were believed to have survived the "Deluge," their take on the divine flood. Umbri communities constructed some of the land's first temples in rural areas, devvoted to Minerva, Clitumnus, Feronia, and other Umbrian deities. The Eugubian Tablets, recovered centuries later, revealed carvings written in the ancient Umbrian language that hinted at animal sacrifices and other early religious rituals. Despite their seniority over the tribes, they would become overwhelmed during later Roman invasions, and either broke up into even smaller villages or merged with nearby communities.

Much of the birth and development of early Rome, however, is indebted to an advanced people that lived northwest of Old Latium known as the "Etruscans." The Etruscan community, which existed between the 8th century and the 2nd century BCE, had a culture largely molded by the Greek presence in Italy, and it was certainly a powerful entity. At one point in time, the Etruscans, a "loose confederation of city-states" to the north of Rome, were guarded by the most robust fortifications on the land, with their territories encompassing lands around the Po to the Tiber Rivers at its prime.

The Etruscans had not only mastered the cultivation of their lands, dipping their toes into commerce only fed their expansion. Instead of sitting on their rich abundance of mineral resources, the Etruscans capitalized on their supplies and created a booming market through manufacture and trade. Specializing in iron, fast-talking Etruscan merchants reeled in traders from not only nearby cities, but Mediterranean powers such as the Phoenicians and the Greeks, Baltic lands, Egypt, and other cultures classified under the Near East. In exchange for locally-sourced iron and other metal products, Etruscans received amber from the Baltic; ivory goods, decorated ostrich eggs, jewelry fashioned out of glass paste, bronze boats, and bejeweled scarabs from Egypt, Sardinia, and other cultures of the Near East; as well as pottery and other handmade artifacts from Greece. Business was so good that the Etruscans minted their own gold and silver coins.

It was through frequent trade with the Greeks and other exotic cultures that these foreign elements became infused into Etruscan culture. For starters, they spoke a language entirely different from other Italic tribes, with an alphabet inspired by a variant of the Greek language and supported by a West Semitic writing system. Also like the Greeks, the Etruscans were polytheistic, and paid tribute to a trio of gods and goddesses – Tin, the sky god; Uni, his wife; and the earth goddess, Cel. Grecian gods, such as Menrva (Minerva), Pacha (Dionysus), and Aritimi (Artemis) were later incorporated into the Etruscan belief system.

Some historians believe that the Etruscans, a highly superstitious people, might have originated from Asia Minor, particularly due to their practice of augury. Augury was fortunetelling, a divine reading of the will of the gods through bird-watching, or the investigation of animal viscera. Other archaeologists have detected traces of Asian culture in some of their ancient language, their trademark pointed shoes, and their love for arches.

Either way, this early melting pot of a tribe descended upon and captured the walled Italic cities of Rome midway through the 7th century BCE, taking the constellation of unrefined clay huts with patchy straw roofs and marrying them to create a unified city – one that would soon become an indomitable force of an empire.

It would only be a matter of time before Roman civilization, which bordered Etruscan territory, absorbed its culture. To begin with, Roman religion, much like that of the Etruscans, revolved around an array of gods and goddesses who could be swayed into interfering with human affairs through sacrifice and other religious rituals. Roman pagans themselves more than dabbled in augury; their priests also possessed sacred texts disclosed to them by the gods and Etruscan sages.

The Etruscan language is also considered an ancestor of the Latin tongue. In fact, Latin has lifted quite a few words straight out of the Etruscan books, such as *"fasces,"* a weapon carried by magisterial attendants featuring an ax blade projecting from a bundle of elmwood, and the *"toga palmata,"* a magistrate's robe. Wealthy Romans of the time understood the significance of Etruscan education and enrolled their children in both Etruscan and Greek institutes.

Etruscan culture would also leave its enduring imprints on the societal and Christian cultures of Rome. Gladiators brawling until only one was left standing during the funerals for Etruscan nobles was a custom that would later become one of the most distinguishable earmarks of ancient Roman tradition. Depictions of Christian demons and fallen angels were said to have resembled Etruscan demons, and early Roman art and literature were also said to have been heavily seasoned with Etruscan elements.

Most pivotal of the Etruscan influence on Roman civilization was their impact on the infrastructure of the villages, as well as the molding of the Roman governing system and its political values. Before the arrival of the Etruscans, the major settlements on the 7 hills of Rome – the Palatine, Aventine, Campidoglio, Esquiline, Quirinal, Viminal, and Caelian Hills – were cordoned off by their borders and conflicting customs, and as a result, mostly kept to themselves. That was, until the Etruscans introduced an annual region-wide festival that would bring the previously hesitant inhabitants of all hills together.

The *Septimontium* was not only the name of the complex of villages sprinkled throughout the seven "*montes*," it also referred to the religious festival all the villagers participated in. Due to the time frame, little information has survived about these celebrations. Chroniclers believe the villagers gathered to pay homage to Apollo, the "Laurel-bearing sun god" with chariot races, plays, and sacred tokens of the people's gratitude. Following an animated procession enlivened by singing, dancing, and other forms of merriment around the Palatine and Esquiline Hills, the villagers convened at the former hill for a special sacrifice. Authorities cleared out large sections of the streets and forbade the use of chariots and other vehicles to make room for the procession. The sacrifice, known as a *"palatuar,"* was conducted by a "bare-headed" pagan priest they called the *"flamen palatualis."*

Offering "sparkling grains of pure salt" and the "mate of a woolly ewe" slain and neatly gutted by the sacrificial butcher *(agones),* as well as other symbolic gifts, the villagers hoped for blessings of good weather and bountiful harvests from the gods. Other reports of gifts given include gilded statues, such as an ox and a pair of goats for Apollo, and a heifer for Apollo's mother, Leto. Afterwards, some Roman emperors presented senators and knights with baskets brimming with loaves of bread and hunks of meat; miniature versions of these baskets were also doled out to the masses. The festival of the *Septimontium* would become a staple pagan festival that Roman Christians would later adamantly refuse to partake in.

Arguably the most successful of the *Septimontium* team-building activities were the series of games developed especially for the festival, known as the *"Ludi*

Apollinares," or the "Apollo Games." These games were said to have been paid for through taxes acquired from village treasuries, and donations fished from the public. These games took up the majority of the festival's repertoire. They included the *Ludi Scaenici,* a collection of religious plays, mimes, and dances dedicated to the sun gods, the *Ludi Circenses,* the spirited chariot races (later held in the Circus Maximus), and running races, wrestling matches, and other recreational tests of skill. Livy, a Roman historian from the 1st century BCE, summed up the bustling atmosphere of the *Septimontium* festival: "All the people took part in them [wore] wreaths of flowers. The married women offered prayers. The doors to the houses were opened, meals eaten in the open, and the day marked with every observance..."

It was supposedly through the *Septimontium* that the villages on the hills learned to work as a cohesive unit. The villagers collaborated to drain the low-lying marshy grounds between the hills to the best of their abilities. They transformed these uninhabitable and "malarial" lands into markets where all the villagers could trade, which only strengthened the trust and new political bridges built between these villages. Through the guidance of the Etruscan elite, which instilled in them the concept of a monarchy and the tools to build this centralized form of government, the scattered villages of

Rome were soon compressed into one city.

Rome emerged as an official city-state of its own under Etruscan rule. They were buttressed by an initially modest, but soon-to-be stellar military, with much of the training and battle techniques passed onto them by the Etruscans. During spells of strife and dances with disaster, the villagers, now citizens under the same government, learned to pool their resources together to aid their fellow countrymen.

The Etruscans are also credited with planting the seeds for what Rome would become most recognizable for: the structurally sound and phenomenal urban infrastructure seemingly eons ahead of its time. The city's aqueducts, underground sewer system, public baths, smooth stone roads, and durable bridges were said to have been modeled after Etruscan blueprints. The Etruscans also helped to boost Roman trade, and discovered ways to enhance the fields of agriculture and the local metal production.

By the 5th century BCE, Rome had landed on the map as one of the mightiest and most influential cities in all of Old Latium, and ironically, all the assistance and resources the Etruscans had parted with would ultimately contribute to their own demise. The Roman armies grew more potent and were soon assertive enough to conquer the last of its neighbors, thereby enlarging the republic.

Once they had triumphed in convincing the Latin villagers to revolt against its leaders and join forces with the republic, the Romans homed in on the Etruscans, whom historians say "lacked a strong national identity." As enterprising as the Etruscans were, those envious of them found a crucial flaw in the disorganization of the multiple governments within Etruria. Some cities were guarded by scores of soldiers, but a large chunk of them were untrained and barely older than the armors on their bodies. While other Etruscan cities had managed to get their hands on veteran troops, they were outnumbered by Greek and Roman soldiers, many of the latter trained by the Etruscan veterans themselves.

In 506 BCE, an alliance of Latins and Greeks from Cumae in South Italy, their biggest competitor in sea power and commerce, conquered Etruscan troops. The Etruscans, gravely crippled, were left vulnerable to being squeezed out of the trade routes on both land and sea. Before long, the reins to the Romans had also slipped from the Etruscan grasp. By 400 BCE, Rome had become an independent institution, rebranded itself as the "Roman Republic," and could now prepare themselves for expansion.

Unusual Medical Practices

Rome was an ancient society with limited technology, so anyone who got sick or seriously injured was often in trouble. Given what they had to work with, Roman doctors tried a variety of practices to cure the sick, and inevitably, many of them seem quite odd by modern standards.

For example, those suffering from eye ailments would be treated with a plaster made up of egg yolk and ground-up flies. This was recommended by no less a figure than Galen, the great doctor of the 3rd century CE, who was so respected that his eye cure continued to be used well into the 18th century. Another Roman cure for sore eyes that didn't last so long was to soothe them with boiled liver.

The Romans even tried to conjure up a cure for acne by rubbing the spots with crocodile meat. Meanwhile, warts could be cured by burning calves' dung and waving the warty area through the smoke. One had to hope the wart wasn't near the nose. Epileptics were advised to eat dried camel brain soaked in vinegar, and those suffering from gout, an inflammation of the joints, needed only to touch a menstruating woman in order to feel better. One could cure headaches by soaking a cloth in menstrual blood and rose oil and applying it to the forehead.

Part of the reason for this profusion of odd remedies was

that Roman physicians could not agree on what caused disease. Galen lived through the Roman Empire's worst pandemic, the Antonine Plague, but physicians at the time had no knowledge of bacteria and viruses (smallpox is a virus, *Variola*), but they did know how contagion arose and spread. According to Galen, Hippocrates, and other Greco-Roman authorities, pestilence was caused by *miasma*, foul air produced by the decomposition of organic matter. Though modern scientists have since been able to disprove this, on the face of it there was some logic to the idea. Physicians and philosophers (they were very often the same, Galen being an example) noticed that disease arose in areas of poor sanitation, where filth and rotting matter was prevalent and not disposed of, and the basic measures to prevent disease – waste removal, provision of clean food and water and quarantining - would have been obvious to them. The scenting of miasmic air with incense and other unguents to expel the foulness would also have thus made sense, though people now know that can't stop the spread of a disease.

Ancient physicians at the time believed that *miasma* was not the direct cause of disease but rather a catalyst. Maladies were caused by an imbalance of what Galen called the four humors. According to him (and Hippocrates before him), the body contained four kinds of fluids: black bile, yellow bile, blood, and phlegm. These corresponded to the four elements of which the entire universe was composed: earth, fire, water, and air. Black bile was tied to earth, yellow bile to fire, blood to air, and phlegm to water. It was believed that the balance of the humors in the body not only determined an individual's health, but their behavior and temperament as well. A melancholic (from *melanos*, the word for "black") disposition was caused by an excess of black bile. Yellow bile made a person fiery or choleric (from *khole*, the word for bile), while a phlegmatic (from *phlegma*, body moisture) temperament denoted a surplus of phlegm. The most desirable temperament was the sanguine (*sanguis*, blood), which exhibited happiness, calm and enthusiasm. The ancient Romans thought *miasma* caused an imbalance in these fluids, and disease resulted. For the ancient physician, as indeed for all physicians for the next 1,500 years or so, illness was not the direct result of external agents.

The theory of the four humors was based on philosophy rather than what today would be called science. It might seem easy to ridicule the idea in hindsight, but the ancient philosophers and doctors did not and could not possess the elementary scientific knowledge that medical practitioners have today, so humorism can be seen as an honest attempt to make sense of the human body and its malignancies.

That said, some of the other beliefs held by Galen and

like-minded physicians are perhaps less understandable. For example, he held that blood was produced by the liver and that it did not circulate through the heart. He also believed that phlegm was produced in the brain. In his defense, Galen was not permitted to dissect cadavers, so his anatomical knowledge came mostly from the dissection of animals and the examination of wounds. Roman law forbade the dissection of human corpses because it was considered impious and an affront to the gods, who had created the human form in a state of perfection. When Christianity became the state religion in the 4th century, the prohibition remained for the same reason: the dignity of a human being created by God, and especially sanctified by baptism, demanded that its body remain intact.[1] That proscription hampered the study of medicine for centuries.

In light of the humor theory, Galen's approach to the pestilence hinged on him being able to identify the imbalance of fluids in the bodies of the victims. In other words, he had to determine which humor predominated in those afflicted. Galen wrote extensively about the symptoms of plague victims, but not much about the treatment. The vomiting of dry blood (thought to be bile) and eruption of pustules described by Galen permit the speculation that the disease was caused by an excess of

---

[1] Though some dissections did occur during medieval times.

bile, and indeed, bile was considered the most noxious of the humors.[2] Humorist theory held that all the humors were present in the blood, so to aid the release of harmful humors, physicians often made an incision to allow blood to drain. This practice, known as bloodletting, was not believed to be dangerous if controlled, as Galen believed that blood was formed in the liver and did not circulate. Despite the fact it didn't work (and often hurt the patient), bloodletting would be practiced well into the 19th century.

Diet was considered the first avenue to restoring the balance of the humors. The adage "you are what you eat" struck especially true for the ancient physician, who believed that certain foods could augment or counter the effects of particular humors. Yellow bile was associated with high temperatures and dryness, black bile with coldness and dryness, phlegm with wet and cold, and blood with heat and moisture. As a result, an excess of black bile might then be treated with foods considered hot, such as garlic, onions, meat and olives.

The emphasis on an appropriate diet probably helped a lot of ill persons, albeit in a somewhat inadvertent and haphazard way. For example, the prescription of only clear, unpolluted water (mountain water was the best)[3]

---

[2] Amir Arsalan Afkhami (2012) "Humoralism" *Encyclopaedia Iranica*
   http://www.iranicaonline.org/articles/humoralism-1
[3] David K. Osborn (2008) "Diet" Food and drink*" Greek Medicine.net*
   http://www.greekmedicine.net/hygiene/Diet_Food_and_Drink.html

would have not only been beneficial to the patient, but would have assisted in the prevention of contagion, though physicians didn't know the real reasons why.

In the end, Galen was unable to stem the tide of the pestilence, but he could predict the outcome of the disease, noting that all who developed a black rash usually survived. The few notes that survive indicate that he paid great attention to the observation of the symptoms and to reason, and though his philosophical principles were erroneous, his commonsense approach and empathy must surely have provided some relief and comfort to many suffering from the disease.

Other doctors proposed other causes for diseases. Crinas of Massalia (1st century CE), who (like many Romans) was fascinated with astrology, thought disease came from the stars. Columella, another 1st century CE doctor, came closer to the truth by proposing that illness came from poisonous vapors arising from swamps. Because of this belief, the Romans drained the Codetan swamp near Rome, thereby reducing malaria, and other swamps located near settlements were drained too. Marcus Terentius Varro (116-27 BCE) made the right guess by saying disease came from tiny creatures invisible to the human eye that floated in the air and entered the body through the nose and mouth, but he lacked the technology to prove his theory.

These many strange practices and beliefs should not blind people to the real medical advances that were developed in ancient Rome. While they had a much different view of the world, Roman physicians did have a good knowledge of some medical herbs with actual curative properties. Garlic was a favorite, and that has been shown to be a mild antibiotic as well as reducing inflammation. Yarrow root was another natural antiseptic, as was honey. Teas made with marshmallow root and horehound were good for a cough. Cabbage was prescribed for constipation. This high-fiber plant would have certainly been useful, but the Romans missed the mark in not noticing that many foods are high in fiber.

Physicians could also perform basic surgery such as splinting a broken leg and even removing cataracts. One of the more interesting medical treatments was an effective form of birth control (the wondrous plant *silphium* is covered further below in the section on sex), and if a woman died in childbirth, the baby could often be saved through Caesarean section, which got its name from the long-held belief that Julius Caesar or an ancestor of his was born in this way.

Much of Rome's medical knowledge came from the Greeks, who had a long history of medical research and provided the empire with some of its best physicians, but the Romans built on this with several innovations of their own. Forbidden by Roman law from dissecting human beings, even foreign slaves, the great physician Galen took to dissecting monkeys, and he was quick to realize that they are people's closest relatives in the animal kingdom. When monkeys were hard to come by, he experimented on live pigs. One of his discoveries was how the spinal cord brings messages to the body. By cutting the spinal cord at various places, he could inflict varying levels of paralysis on the poor pigs.

Like surgeons throughout history, Galen also found ways around the law against human vivisection. He admitted to dissecting a hanged criminal, as well as several putrefied bodies that washed out of a cemetery during a flood. Galen got his early training at a school for gladiators. While he didn't get to dissect the losers, he did get a chance to study various types of wounds, and probably more than a few internal organs in a less-than-pristine state.

The Romans stressed preventative medicine and urged people to take regular baths, although the public bath houses did not change the water nearly enough. Roman culture also stressed regular exercise and a good diet. Some individuals, such as Emperor Vespasian (r. 69–79 CE), practiced intermittent fasting. Public latrines, where people sat in rows wiping their backsides with sponges, were cleaned regularly. Teams of slaves were also assigned the task of cleaning the streets of refuse and the large amount of animal droppings that accumulated in any settlement.

Despite Rome having better medical care than most other ancient civilizations, Pliny the Elder did not have good things to say about physicians in his seminal work, *Natural History*. He wrote, "The medical profession is the only one in which anybody professing to be a physician is at once trusted, although nowhere else is an untruth more dangerous. We pay however no attention to the danger, so great for each of us is the seductive sweetness of wishful thinking. Besides this, there is no law to punish criminal ignorance, no instance of retribution. Physicians acquire their knowledge from our dangers, making experiments at the cost of our lives. Only a physician can commit homicide with complete impunity."

Odd Eating Habits

One thing that was quite unique about the Romans was their cuisine. While the common people had a repetitive diet of bread, porridge, fruits, and vegetables in season, and occasionally fish and meat, the wealthy had an eclectic range of dishes to tempt them. Food was imported from all parts of the empire to create a truly incredible variety, and Roman cuisine emphasized contrasts - sweet mixed with salty, bitter mixed with savory - to create flavor combinations that would put a modern restaurant out of business after its first weekend.

The Romans generally ate in the manner of the Mediterranean countries today. A light breakfast called a *ientaculum* would be served at dawn, followed by a heavy lunch called a *cena*, which was the main meal of the day and served in the early afternoon. At nightfall, they had a moderately-sized supper called the *vesperna*. A brunch (*prandium*) could be added for those who were hungrier.

One favorite dish was *garum*, a sauce made from fish innards. *Garum* was a staple for anyone who had any spare money, but those who have reproduced it according to old records generally agree that it tastes disgusting, which should come as no surprise considering how it was made. Salted fish intestines crushed up to make a viscous liquid would be allowed to evaporate down to a thick, salty paste. The Romans loved the strong flavor and put it on all sorts of dishes, thus including it in various recipes.

Each city had its own recipe for producing *garum*, and naturally they used different varieties of local fish, so there was a lot of local pride and intense competition between cities. The *garum* produced in Hispania and Lusitania was some of the most popular and got exported across the Roman world.

A similar dish was *liquamen*. The recipe is known from a

10th century Byzantine manuscript on agriculture titled *Geoponica*. It reads, "The intestines of fish are thrown into a vessel, and are salted; and small fish, especially *atherinae*, or small mullets, or *maenae*, or *lycostomi*, or any small fish, are all salted in the same manner; and they are seasoned in the sun, and frequently turned; and when they have been seasoned in the heat, the *garum* is thus taken from them. A small basket of close texture is laid in the vessel filled with the small fish already mentioned, and the *garum* will flow into the basket; and they take up what has been percolated through the basket, which is called *liquamen*; and the remainder of the feculence is made into *allec*."

   Perhaps the most famous Roman dish was the dormouse. These little rodents are featured in countless novels and movies about the Romans, being seen so often that Dr. Mary Beard came up with the "Dormouse test," in which the historical accuracy of a fictional work is in inverse proportion to how quickly one of the characters eats dormice.

   Be that as it may, the Romans did indeed eat the fat little rodents, or at least the wealthy did. They were rather expensive, and the larger ones were especially prized. Some rich hosts would even show off their generosity by having their dormice weighed at the table before being served to guests.

Dormice featured in a variety of recipes. They were often roasted, dipped in honey, or stuffed with a variety of nuts and meat. They would be captured in autumn when they were at their heaviest and kept in captivity while being fed on a rich diet of nuts to fatten them up even further.

Other dishes included exotic imports such as ostrich and camel. The more unusual the animal, the more it was in demand for Roman diners.

Those who lived by the sea were big fans of seafood. Besides the usual fish, shellfish, and octopi, Romans ate the stranger creatures of the sea, such as anemones and sea urchins. These spiky dishes were dangerous to eat, and archaeologists studying ancient coprolites (preserved feces) have discovered spines that had passed through the Romans' bodies.

While there are many strange true facts about the Romans, there are also plenty of myths. One is the *vomitorium*. This was purported to be a special room where people could go to purge themselves before starting a second round of overeating. In fact, *vomitorium* is a term for the entrance doors to theaters and amphitheaters connecting the lobbies to the tiers of seats. The word comes from the fact that these doorways spewed forth large crowds of people, a bit like an overfed Roman spewing forth sea urchins. The *Dictionary of Roman and Greek Antiquities* by Anthony Rich (1893) noted, "It is calculated that the Flavian amphitheatre was capable of containing more than 90,000 spectators, and was fitted with vomitories and staircases sufficient for the whole concourse to disperse in less than five minutes."

Strange Religious and Magical Practices

Religion was an intimate part of Roman culture and was performed on two levels. There were the official temples and festivals sponsored by the state for the major gods, and then there were various folk festivals and minor deities, many of them imported from conquered lands and celebrated by the common people. There were also gods of the home, as well as the more universal gods worshipped in the home. Generally, the head of this worship was the man of the house, who acted as a kind of priest for his family. Both elite and common folks alike paid close attention to auguries and consulted oracles.

This patchwork of different beliefs had no unifying philosophy, which is probably why philosophers were so much more prominent in the ancient world than they are today. One historian noted that instead of having a theology, Romans had various methods for making deals with the divine and supernatural to try and affect things beyond their control. This could lead to some odd beliefs.

Festivals were an important part of the Roman calendar, and every month had them. There were those celebrated across the empire, and then those celebrated only in certain localities or by followers of a certain cult. Many of the festivals went back to the mists of prehistory. For example, the *lupercalia* in February was associated with the god Faunus and was a fertility festival that sounds like something more suited to a primitive tribe than a growing urban empire. The ritual started in the cave in Rome where Romulus and Remus were said to have been suckled by the she-wolf. Priests would sacrifice several goats and a dog and smear the blood on the faces of two young patrician boys. The boys were dressed in goatskins and carried strips of leather in their hands. Once properly smeared with blood, they'd run along a predetermined course whipping anyone who got in their way. Getting whipped was supposed to help with fertility, so women who wanted to get pregnant would deliberately get in the boys' way. No doubt the boys enjoyed this ritual thoroughly.

A more refined festival was that dedicated to Vesta, which took up a full week in June. Vesta was one of the great goddesses of the Roman state, and all official business would be suspended during this week. The temple would open up to married women so they could come in and sacrifice food to this goddess of the hearth.

On the first day of the festival, June 9, mill donkeys would be given a day of rest. These were horribly abused animals, tethered to a heavy stone mill and forced to walk in circles all day as the mill ground wheat into flour. If they slowed down, they were whipped. They often ended up dying in their tracks, after which their meat was sold off to the local butchers. But for one day, they got a vacation and were garlanded with flowers and loaves of bread.

One Roman religious institution that has been the object of enduring fascination, then and now, was the Vestal Virgins. Counting only six in number, these women, who had taken a vow of chastity, kept the sacred fire lit in the temple of Vesta at the Forum in Rome. They were also on hand for numerous other rituals and festivals throughout the religious year, and they baked a special salt cake that was used in several ceremonies.

The post of Vestal Virgin carried serious responsibilities and great honor. They could be whipped for not fulfilling their duties, and if they had sex they would be walled up alive. A 19th century writer, Anthon Smith, described this in detail: "When condemned by the college of pontifices, she was stripped of her vittae and other badges of office, was scourged, was attired like a corpse, placed in a close litter, and borne through the forum attended by her weeping kindred, with all the ceremonies of a real funeral, to a rising ground called the Campus Sceleratus just within the city walls, close to the Colline gate. There a small vault underground had been previously prepared, containing a couch, a lamp, and a table with a little food. The pontifex maximus, having lifted up his hands to heaven and uttered a secret prayer, opened the litter, led forth the culprit, and placing her on the steps of the ladder which gave access to the subterranean cell, delivered her over to the common executioner and his assistants, who conducted her down, drew up the ladder, and having filled the pit with earth until the surface was level with the surrounding ground, left her to perish deprived of all the tributes of respect usually paid to the spirits of the departed."

This actually happened in 114 BCE, when a young Vestal Virgin named Helvia was struck by lightning while out riding a horse. No surer proof of the displeasure of the gods could be imaginable, and it was decided that she must have broken her vow of chastity because she was found with her clothing hiked up and her private parts showing. Furthermore, her dead horse was missing its trappings.

When the Senate investigated, it heard the testimony of a slave who named three other Vestal Virgins who had been sleeping with men, and they were dealt with in the customary fashion. Also, two foreign couples from Greece and Gaul were buried alive as a sacrifice to foreign spirits. This is a rare example of human sacrifice in the Roman world.

Despite the strict rules, there was a great deal of competition for the post, which brought high honor to the woman's family. It also would appeal to women who did not want to marry, since for patrician families, marriage was generally arranged and not subjected to the vagaries of love. In the year 19 CE, Emperor Tiberius was called upon to choose a new Vestal Virgin from two excellent candidates, both from important families. He decided against one of the candidates, saying that although the girl was just as good as her competitor, since her father was divorced, her family was slightly less pure. As compensation, he gave the losing girl a dowry of a million sesterces, a huge sum.

A Roman statue of a Vestal Virgin

A picture of the Temple of Vesta

Another early festival was dedicated to the goddess Furrina and celebrated on July 25, which had lost its meaning by the middle of the 1st century BCE. No one could remember what Furrina was the goddess of, but Romans were too superstitious to ignore a goddess, no matter how little they knew about her, so they kept performing her festival.

Whatever she had been in the early days, she must have been important, because she was one of the 15 official deities of the Roman Republic, each with its own priest called a *flamen*. There is some evidence that she was associated with springs, but it is unclear just what that association was.

Most studies of Roman religion focus on the big temples in major cities, but the majority of the Roman population lived in the countryside as farmers, and religion was quite different for them. They believed spirits were everywhere, including in the streams, the fields, and the trees. Each place had its *numen*, a vaguely understood spirit that should be honored and propitiated. Boundary stones, called a *terminus* or *termini*, were especially important, as any boundary was a nexus of spiritual power, hence the importance of the doorway in a home.

Early in Rome's history the priesthood named a god

Terminus. The story goes that when the temple of Jupiter was being built on the Capitoline Hill, the workers found a boulder. Try as they might, they couldn't budge it, so it was decided that it was a great god, so great that he couldn't even be moved by Jupiter, king of the gods. The temple was built around the boulder and Terminus was honored thereafter.

In addition to these spirits, there was a variety of more tangible beings such as satyrs and dryads familiar to those who have read mythology. Lesser known was the Mormo, an evil woman with donkey legs who had an appetite for children. Verspilles were werewolves who lived as normal men during the day, only to turn into wolves at night and hunt with packs of real wolves, causing all sorts of mayhem. An odd type of vampire liked to sneak into houses at night and eat men's noses.

Numerous festivals were connected to the agricultural calendar. One, on April 15, honored the earth goddess Tellus. Pregnant cows were sacrificed in her honor and animal fetuses were burned on the altars of her temples. Four days later came the festival of Ceres, the goddess of grain. This goddess was of vital importance because grain was the base of the Roman diet. Farmers would march around the boundaries of their land in a ritual called the *lustration* in order to purify it. In the city of Rome in the early days, foxes would have torches tied to their tails and be let loose in a field where the Circus Maximus was eventually built. The panicked foxes running this way and that with their tails on fire must have been quite a sight.

Another April festival involved sacrificing a red puppy to Robigus, the god of mildew. Robigus was an important god since he protected the fields from grain rot. The puppy had to be red because a common form of grain disease, "wheat rust," left reddish spots on the plant and therefore the dog's color served as a kind of sympathetic magic.

The private home had a profusion of deities. Vesta was honored both in large state temples and at home. The woman of the house would pray to her daily, essentially acting as a domestic Vestal Virgin without the requirement for chastity. At every meal, some food would be thrown in the fire for Vesta to consume.

Janus was the double-faced guard of the doorway. With faces looking in both directions, it could see all and was both inside and outside the home. No fewer than three other deities were involved in protecting the doorway. Limentius looked over the threshold, Forculus was god of door leaves, and even the hinges had its own goddess in the form of Cardea.

Loudon Dodd's picture of a statue of Janus

There were also spirits of dead ancestors honored by small figurines kept in a special cupboard, spirits of the pantry, an overall spirit of the house, and many more. In essence, the Romans believed the whole house was crowded with gods and spirits, and most were benign as long as they were properly honored, but even the most religious householders had to keep up their guard. Ghosts could come into the house and had to be chased off by banging metal pots and spitting out black beans.

There were also gods and goddesses for every stage of life, from conception to birth to learning to talk. When someone in the family died, a figurine was made of them and they were added to the others. The house would be swept, a pig sacrificed to Ceres, and the surviving members of the family stepped across a ceremonial fire and were sprinkled with water in order to be purified.

Romans loved the exotic, and they eagerly embraced the religions of the strange new lands they conquered, adding them to an already well-populated pantheon. This was part of their success, and as long as conquered groups assimilated in this way, accepting Roman rule and (in later years) making sacrifices to the emperor, they were allowed to keep their local gods and customs. There were legendary exceptions to this assimilation, namely the Druids and Jews, both of whom insisted their religion was greater than, not equal to, that of Rome. The religious leaders of the Celts and Judaism were at the forefront of their peoples' resistance to Roman rule, and thus Rome decided they needed to be destroyed.

If a culture did accept assimilation, then they could expect their local traditions to be accepted and their gods to spread around the empire. A remarkable case of this was Egypt, which became part of the empire around 30 BCE in the wake of the Battle of Actium. Rome became fascinated with Egypt's exotic culture and its elaborate rites, its animal-headed deities, and its mummies and pyramids. Before long, Rome was experiencing

Egyptomania, much the same way 19th century Europe did. Rich Romans decorated their gardens in Egyptian themes complete with miniature pyramids, and the cult of Isis became popular among Roman women.

Romans also had a keen interest in auguries. When an animal sacrifice was made to a god or goddess, the animal would be disemboweled and its entrails closely studied. If something strange was found such as a deformity or illness, that was considered a bad omen and another animal would have to be sacrificed. Only an animal with perfect innards was good enough for the gods.

Moreover, different gods demanded different kinds of sacrifice. For example, Mars, being the god of war, was a bit more demanding than most, so the faithful had to sacrifice a sheep, pig, and an ox all together. On October 15, however, a holy day for Mars, there would be a special chariot race and the winning horse, the inside horse of the lead team, would be the sacrifice. As one can see, animal sacrifice could get very expensive, but at least the bulk of the meat would then be eaten at a special feast.

There were other methods for divining the future as well. Priests would study the flights of birds or the patterns of lightning in the sky. Auspices were taken ahead of all major events, such as the birth of a child, the declaration of war, establishing a business, or a long journey. In an uncertain world, Romans wanted some reassurance that they had a bit of control over, or at least knowledge of, the future.

Those who ignored the auspices or did not respect the practice would be subject to swift reprisal by the fates. It was an old practice for the Roman armed forces to bring sacred chickens along with them. When about to make an important decision or maneuver, they would crumble up a cake in front of them. If the chickens ate it, all would be well. If they ignored it, the future looked grim.

Before the Battle of Drepana in 249 BCE, during the first Punic War, the Roman navy faced the Carthaginian navy off the coast of Sicily. The Roman commander, Publius Claudius Pulcher, was enraged when the chickens didn't eat the cake. In a fit he threw them overboard, saying if they wouldn't eat, then they could drink. The Roman navy was subsequently crushed, losing most of their ships and some 20,000 men. He was recalled to Rome, found guilty of impiety and incompetence, and given a hefty fine. He died not long thereafter, and it appears he might have killed himself to avoid a life of disgrace.

An account of Emperor Galba (r. 68-69 CE) explained his destiny for greatness: "When Galba's grandfather was busy with a sacrifice for a stroke of lightning, and an eagle snatched the intestines from his hand and carried them to an oak full of acorns, the prediction was made that the highest dignity would come to the family, but late; whereupon he said with a laugh: 'Very likely, when a mule has a foal.' Afterwards when Galba was beginning his revolt, nothing gave him so much encouragement as the foaling of a mule, and while the rest were horrified and looked on it as an unfavorable omen, he alone regarded it as most propitious, remembering the sacrifice and his grandfather's saying."

The reference to making a sacrifice after a stroke of lightning demonstrates again how the Romans were so superstitious. A lightning strike was considered an ill omen, and a sacrifice would have to be made to placate Jupiter, who hurled lightning when he was angry.

Closely related to religion was magic, in which the mortal tried to imitate the gods by trying a little supernatural power themself. The most enduring evidence for this comes from the *defixiones* (curse tablets). The thin sheets of lead were inscribed with a curse and then rolled up and stuck under the floor, inside wall cavities, or thrown in wells. Given lead's imperishable nature, many have survived into the modern world, and one fragmentary example in the British Museum reads, "I curse Tretia Maria and her life and mind and memory and liver and lungs mixed up together, and her words, thoughts and memory; thus may she be unable to speak what things are concealed, nor be able..." Another says, "The sheet which is given to Mercury, that he exact vengeance for the gloves which have been lost; that he take blood and health from the person who has stolen them; that he provide what we ask the god Mercury ... as quickly as possible for the person who has taken these gloves."

There were also less malign practices, and the Romans utilized many practices to avert bad luck. Many wore charms against the evil eye, such as *fascinus*, which was shaped like an erect penis. Also, the left side was considered evil. The Latin word is *sinistram*, the origin of the English word "sinister." Left-handed people were forced to favor their right, a practice that endured in the West well into the 20th century, and one took care never to cross a threshold with the left foot first.

Pictures of *fascinus*

Some animals were considered unlucky, such as a black cat, and to have one walk into the house was a sure sign of impending disaster. The Romans shared a distaste for snakes with many other cultures, and they were especially afraid if one fell from the roof of the house into the yard.

Other beliefs were even more bizarre. If a Roman was at a banquet and someone mentioned fire, they immediately had to spill water on the table. One can imagine Roman children doing this so their parents would make a mess, although considering the amount of corporal punishment meted out on children in Roman times, perhaps only the more foolish children pulled that prank.

Abuses of Power

Though people are most familiar with the Roman Empire, Rome started as a kingdom, but little is known about this period, and the last king was overthrown in 509 BCE in order to establish a republic. The Roman Republic was ruled by a group of elite families who ran the Senate and occupied all the chief positions, a system that was disrupted by Julius Caesar and technically abolished in 27 BCE by Octavian, who became Rome's first emperor.

This was not entirely a bad thing at the time, since Rome was an expanding empire facing a large number of challenges. A good emperor, buoyed by an entrenched expert bureaucracy, would be a unifying force against enemies without and instability within. Octavian, best known today as Augustus, oversaw the formation of the *Pax Romana*, but it goes without saying that not all of Rome's rulers were as competent as Augustus. The success such rulers had in centralizing the empire's administration, while undoubtedly bringing huge benefits, also sowed the seeds for later problems. After all, as so many Roman emperors proved, from Caligula and Nero to Commodus, the empire's approach to governance was predicated on the ruler's ability. When incompetent or insane emperors came to power, the whole edifice came tumbling down.

A statue of Augustus

One of the most popular sources on the lives of the Roman emperors came from Gaius Suetonius Tranquillus, who wrote *De Vita Caesarum* (*About the Life of the Caesars*). Today, the work is known as *The Twelve Caesars*, and it was written in 121 CE during the reign of the Emperor Hadrian. Suetonius was the emperor's personal secretary.

In his work, Suetonius covered the lives of Rome's leaders, from Julius Caesar to Domitian, lauding some and harshly criticizing others. Of course, Suetonius's work must be seen to be as much political as historical. Working for the present emperor, he was influenced by Hadrian's views. He was also greatly pro-Senate, taking its side in any disputes they had with the first 12 Caesars, and there were many. Nevertheless, much of what he wrote has been corroborated in other sources, and while it's clear he exaggerated in some cases, Suetonius is one of the best sources for the period.

Suetonius had a lot of gossip to relate about Tiberius, who ruled from 14–37 CE. Tiberius started his career as a brilliant general, defeating many of Rome's enemies on its eastern frontier in Europe. When he became emperor, at first he showed a great deal of military and administrative acumen, but later in life he began to show signs of intellectual and moral degradation. In 26, he all but retired from public life, leaving the rule of the empire to scheming underlings while he enjoyed himself in an extensive and ornate pleasure palace on the island of Capri. Suetonius wrote:

> "On retiring to Capri he devised a pleasance for his secret orgies: teams of wantons of both sexes,

selected as experts in deviant intercourse and dubbed analists, copulated before him in triple unions to excite his flagging passions. Its bedrooms were furnished with the most salacious paintings and sculptures, as well as with an erotic library, in case a performer should need an illustration of what was required. Then in Capri's woods and groves he arranged a number of nooks of venery where boys and girls got up as Pans and nymphs solicited outside bowers and grottoes: people openly called this 'the old goat's garden,' punning on the island's name.

"He acquired a reputation for still grosser depravities that one can hardly bear to tell or be told, let alone believe. For example, he trained little boys (whom he termed toddlers) to crawl between his thighs when he went swimming and tease him with their licks and nibbles; and unweaned babies he would put to his organ as though to the breast, being by both nature and age rather fond of this form of satisfaction. Left a painting of Parrhasius's depicting Atalanta pleasuring Meleager with her lips on condition that if the theme displeased him he was to have a million sesterces instead, he chose to keep it and actually hung it in his bedroom. The story is also told that once at a sacrifice, attracted by the acolyte's beauty, he lost control of himself and, hardly waiting for the ceremony to end, rushed him off and debauched him and his brother, the flute-player, too; and subsequently, when they complained of the assault, he had their legs broken.

"How grossly he was in the habit of abusing women even of high birth is very clearly shown by the death of a certain Mallonia. When she was brought to his bed and refused most vigorously to submit to his lust, he turned her over to the informers, and even when she was on trial he did not cease to call out and ask her 'whether she was sorry'; so that finally she left the court and went home, where she stabbed herself, openly upbraiding the ugly old man for his obscenity. Hence a stigma put upon him at the next plays in an Atellan farce was received with great applause and became current, that 'the old goat was licking the does.'"

It's difficult to know how much truth there is to these rumors. Unfortunately, some Romans were not averse to this sort of behavior if it was kept reasonably circumspect and did not interfere with one's civic and marital duties. Where Tiberius's fault lay was in not performing the duties of his office, allowing all sorts of scheming and infighting back in Rome instead of keeping the city and the empire under a strong hand. One wonders how much Suetonius would have reported Tiberius's various sexual adventures if he had actually taken his office seriously.

A bust of Tiberius

   Tiberius died at nearly 78 under rather grim circumstances. The historian Tacitus related in his *Annals*, "On the 15th of March, his breath failing, he was believed to have expired, and Gaius Caesar was going forth with a numerous throng of congratulating followers to take the first possession of the empire, when suddenly news came that Tiberius was recovering his voice and sight, and calling for persons to bring him food to revive him from his faintness. Then ensued a universal panic, and while the rest fled hither and thither, every one feigning grief or ignorance, Gaius Caesar, in silent stupor, passed from the highest hopes to the extremity of apprehension. Macro, nothing daunted, ordered the old emperor to be smothered under a huge heap of clothes, and all to quit the entrance-hall."

  Gaius Caesar was none other than Gaius Julius Caesar Augustus Germanicus, who had been named after Caesar and his famous father, the military hero Germanicus. When the boy was only two-years-old, Germanicus had Gaius travel with his legions to Germania, and by all accounts, he was spoiled by the soldiers in camp. Germanicus had the young boy dressed up in a miniature version of full military regalia, right down to baby-sized *caligae*, the tough infantryman's boots. Being extremely taken with this, the soldiers took to calling him Caligula, meaning "little *caligae*," or "little sandals", and the nickname has remained with him ever since. For his part, Caligula was never fond of the nickname, and it was almost certainly never said to his face when he grew older. That's no surprise, given that it would've been a grave breach of form to call even the most benevolent ruler "little sandals," let alone to say it to a man as unstable as Caligula.

Picture of a *caliga* taken by Matthias Kabel

Given how bad some of Rome's emperors were, it's a testament to just how insane and reviled Caligula was that he is still remembered nearly 2,000 years later as the epitome of everything that could be wrong with a tyrant. The Romans had high hopes for him after he succeeded Tiberius in 37 CE, and by all accounts he was a noble and just ruler during his first few months in power. But after that, he suffered some sort of mysterious illness that apparently rendered him insane. Indeed, the list of Caligula's strange actions is long. Among other things, Caligula began appearing in public dressed as gods and goddesses, and his incest, sexual perversion, and thirst for blood were legendary at the time, difficult accomplishments considering Roman society was fairly accustomed to and tolerant of such things.

In fact, the Romans were so taken aback by some of Caligula's behavior that historians catalogued some of his strangest antics. Suetonius wrote that as Caligula's relationship with the Senate deteriorated, he ordered that Incitatus be made a member of the Roman Senate and a Consul. Incitatus, Latin for "swift," was Caligula's favorite horse, but far from simply being a way to stick it to the Senate, Caligula invited guests to dine with Incitatus and had the horse's stables made of marble.

Caligula is the man who had incestuous relationships with virtually every female member of his family, threatened to make his horse a Senator (and did make the horse a priest), and built a bridge of boats connecting two ends of a bay for no other reason than that he wished to ride across water. While there are apparently at least kernels of truth to all these legends, it is worth remembering that, no matter how absurd his excesses, Caligula was a real man who did not behave the way he did in an effort to be a cartoonish caricature of an evil villain. It seems unlikely that Caligula's psychosis was a consequence of a particularly unhealthy family upbringing, a common cause of mental illness. His father was a well-respected man who doted on his little boy, and his mother was a noblewoman who did not display any abusive behaviour. Instead, it seems that Caligula fell prey to a debilitating disease that literally made him go crazy. While Caligula's life and exploits have become the stuff of legends, and his worst excesses are portrayed colorfully and at times almost humorously, the fact that a mental illness seemed to turn a decent ruler into history's biggest madman also makes Caligula a somewhat tragic figure.

Caligula, like most tyrants of his ilk, died prematurely and violently. Perhaps it's surprising that he lasted so long in the first place. Unlike other Roman emperors who were personally despicable and loathed by those aware of their private activities, Caligula managed to alienate the public as well. Moreover, while Caligula was almost certainly mentally ill, the behavior of his sisters was also remarkably sociopathic. It is unclear to what extent they were willing participants in his excesses, or whether they were simply afraid for their lives, but Agrippina the Younger cannot claim fear as the motivation for her acts. Even after Caligula's death, she continued to engage in all kinds of sadistic and immoral acts, including poisoning her husband Claudius to bring her son Nero to power.

Caligula's legend has grown over the centuries, but the facts behind the legend, which are just as outlandish as the stories they inspired, appear to be firmly grounded in truth. Unlike Nero, whose enmity towards Christians was a significant influence on religious-based histories of him, or Commodus, who had the misfortune to follow in the footsteps of one of the greatest minds in Western philosophy (Marcus Aurelius), it does not appear as though the Romans held any bias against Caligula. Seneca, one of the very few surviving contemporary sources of the notorious emperor, had no cause to love him since he was nearly put to death for his alleged involvement in a conspiracy, but other writers like Suetonius cast him as evil and lunacy incarnate. Caligula succeeded the vastly (albeit rather unfairly) disliked Tiberius, he was from the same family as the beloved Julius Caesar and Augustus, the common people did not suffer unduly because of his policies, and he did not suffer any grievous military reverses. Therefore, it is reasonable to assume that everything currently known about Caligula, including even the most lurid stories, is at the very least based somewhat on fact.

A bust of Caligula

Nero ranks among the very worst of the Caesars, alongside the likes of mad Caligula, slothful Commodus, and paranoid Domitian, a figure so hated that, in many ancient Christian traditions, he is literally, without hyperbole, considered the Antichrist; according to a notable Biblical scholar, the coming of the Beast and the number 666 in the Book of Revelation are references to Nero. He was the man who, famously, "fiddled while Rome burned", an inveterate lecher, a murderous tyrant who showed little compunction in murdering his mother and who liked to use Christian martyrs as a source of illumination at night – by burning them alive. His economic policies, according to many historians, virtually bankrupted Rome.

Even his appearance, apparently, was unattractive. His busts show him to be fleshy-faced, with a weak chin that he attempted to disguise with a distinctly unprepossessing beard, and according to Suetionius he was also spotty, stinking, pot-bellied and thin-legged.

The best-known accounts of Nero come from biographers like Tacitus, Cassius Dio, Suetonius and Josephus, but there are also indications that, to some extent, reports of Nero's cruelty were exaggerated. Nero was popular with the common people and much of the army, and during his reign the Empire enjoyed a period of remarkable peace and stability. Many historians, including some of his ancient biographers – such as Josephus – suggest that there existed a strong bias against Nero. Part of this is because his successors wished to discredit him, and justify the insurrections which eventually drove him, hounded from the throne, to a lonely suicide. Much of the bias against Nero can also be attributed to the fact that he was a renowned persecutor of Christians, and since many of the historians who wrote about Nero in the years after his death were Christians themselves, it made sense for them to have a jaundiced view of their erstwhile nemesis. Because of this, some historians have suggested that

Nero's demeanor and reputation might not be as black as the original sources might be inclined to suggest.

Suetonius also recounts many strange omens regarding the emperors, including in the tumultuous Year of the Four Emperors (69 CE), during which the throne passed from Galba, who had taken power the year before, to Otho, Vitellius, and eventually Vespasian. While Vespasian comes off well in Suetonius's work except for his infamous greed, the same cannot be said for the other three.

Things started strangely with the death of Nero in 68. According to Suetonius, "The race of the Caesars ended with Nero. That this would be so was shown by many portents and especially by two very significant ones. Years before, as Livia was returning to her estate near Veii, immediately after her marriage with Augustus, an eagle which flew by dropped into her lap a white hen, holding in its beak a sprig of laurel, just as the eagle had carried it off. Livia resolved to rear the fowl and plant the sprig, whereupon such a great brood of chickens was hatched that to this day the villa is called Ad Gallinas, and such a grove of laurel sprang up, that the Caesars gathered their laurels from it when they were going to celebrate triumphs. Moreover, it was the habit of those who triumphed to plant other branches at once in that same place, and it was observed that just before the death of each of them the tree which he had planted withered. Now in Nero's last year the whole grove died from the root up, as well as all the hens. Furthermore, when shortly afterwards the temple of the Caesars was struck by lightning, the heads fell from all the statues at the same time, and his sceptre, too, was dashed from the hand of Augustus."

Servius Galba, the man who would succeed him, was at the time serving as governor of Hispania Tarraconensis, the northeastern half of the Iberian Peninsula. Already in his 70s, he had a long career as a politician and governor and had shown a cruel streak when it came to dealing with criminals, but his mental powers seemed to have been failing him as he reached his twilight, perhaps due to fatigue from a bad case of hernia and arthritis. Suetonius wrote of him, "For eight years he governed the province in a variable and inconsistent manner. At first he was vigorous and energetic and even over severe in punishing offences; for he cut off the hands of a money-lender who carried on his business dishonestly and nailed them to his counter; crucified a man for poisoning his ward, whose property he was to inherit in case of his death; and when the man invoked the law and declared that he was a Roman citizen, Galba, pretending to lighten his punishment by some consolation and honour, ordered that a cross much higher than the rest and painted white be set up, and the man transferred to it. But he gradually changed to sloth and inaction, not to give Nero any cause for jealousy, and as he used to say himself, because no one could be forced to render an account for doing nothing."

A bust of Galba

When he heard of the death of Nero, and the scheming of other leading men to take the role of emperor, he was encouraged by some predictions in his youth that he would take the purple as an old man. There were also some favorable omens coming at the same time as the news of Nero's death. According to Suetonius, "He was encouraged too, in addition to most favorable auspices and omens, by the prediction of a young girl of high birth, and the more so because the priest of Jupiter at Clunia, directed by a dream, had found in the inner shrine of his temple the very same prediction, likewise spoken by an inspired girl two hundred years before. And the purport of the verses was that one day there would come forth from Spain the ruler and lord of the world."

He was also encouraged by a ship washing ashore, its crew all gone and its hold filled with weapons. Surely that meant he would be victorious in battle. One man's tragedy was another man's victory.

Galba gathered an army and marched for Rome as many would-be emperors would before and after him. More legions rallied to his cause as he went, and he entered the capital unopposed. His reign, however, would only last seven months before he was assassinated in response to a series of unpopular decrees such as seizing property from Roman citizens and disbanding the German legions. Suetonius listed some omens: "Many prodigies in rapid succession from the very beginning of his reign had foretold Galba's end exactly as it happened. When victims were being slain to right and left all along his route in every town, an ox, maddened by the stroke of an axe, broke its bonds and charged the emperor's chariot, and as it raised its feet, deluged him with blood. And as Galba dismounted, one of his guards, pushed forward by the crowd, almost wounded him with his lance. Again, as he entered the city, and later the Palace, he was met by a shock of earthquake and a sound like the lowing of kine. There followed even clearer signs. He had set apart from all the treasure a necklace fashioned of pearls and precious stones, for the adornment of his image of Fortune at Tusculum. This on a sudden impulse he consecrated to the Capitoline Venus, thinking it worthy of a more august position. The next night Fortune appeared to him in his dreams, complaining of being robbed of the gift intended for her and threatening in her turn to take away what she had bestowed. When Galba hastened in terror to Tusculum at daybreak, to offer expiatory sacrifices because of the dream, and sent on men to make preparations for the ceremony, he found on the altar nothing but warm ashes and beside it an old man dressed in black, holding the incense in a glass dish and the wine in an earthen cup. It was also remarked that as he was sacrificing on the Kalends of January, the garland fell from his head, and that as he took the auspices, the sacred chickens flew away. As he was on the point of addressing the soldiers on the day of the adoption, his camp chair, through the forgetfulness of his attendants, was not placed on the tribunal, as is customary, and in the Senate his curule chair was set wrong side foremost."

Galba was ultimately slaughtered by some of his own troops, who proclaimed Otho as emperor. They could have made a better choice, because even at a young age Otho had a mean streak. Suetonius explained, "From earliest youth he was so extravagant and wild that his father often flogged him; and they say that he used to rove about at night and lay hands on any one whom he met who was feeble or drunk and toss him in a blanket."

A bust of Otho

Otho grew up into a wily politician, however, getting to be one of Nero's favorites, at least until Nero took a fancy to Otho's wife and got rid of him by banishing him to the province of Lusitania (roughly modern Portugal), where he served well as governor for 10 years. When Galba became emperor, Otho tried to be named his successor. Galba, however, chose another man, and Otho started to plot against him.

As soon as Galba was out of the way, the bad omens started. Suetonius wrote, "He had a fearful dream that night, uttered loud groans, and was found by those who ran to his aid lying on the ground beside his couch; that he tried by every kind of expiatory rite to propitiate the shade of Galba, by whom he dreamt that he was ousted and thrown out; and that next day, as he was taking the auspices, a great storm arose and he had a bad fall."

Others noted the omens too and felt Otho was ripe for the plucking. The legions in Germany swore allegiance to their general Aulus Vitellius, and he marched on Rome. After they dealt Otho's army a serous defeat, Otho gave up hope and killed himself after ruling only three months.

Suetonius had little good to say about the short-serving emperor except for his mode of death, an honorable one in Roman culture: "Neither Otho's person nor his bearing suggested such great courage. He is said to have been of moderate height, splay-footed and bandy-legged, but almost feminine in his care of his person. He had the hair of his body plucked out, and because of the thinness of his locks wore a wig so carefully fashioned and fitted to his head, that no one suspected it. Moreover, they say that he used to shave every day and smear his face with moist bread, beginning the practice with the appearance of the first down, so as never to have a beard; also that he used to celebrate the rites of Isis publicly in the linen garment prescribed by the cult. I am inclined to think that it was because of these habits that a death so little in harmony with his life excited the greater marvel."

Vitellius was the third man to become emperor that year, but he would not be the last, and the Romans believed (at least in retrospect) that he was dogged by bad omens from the very day he was born. His parents had an astrologer do the infant's horoscope (a common practice), and it proved so negative that his parents tried to keep him out of politics to avoid disaster. But he rose in the ranks anyway, at first showing some ability although later becoming corrupt and dissolute, preferring to stuff his face at rich banquets four times a day than to take part in the hard work of ruling. To keep up such a heavy round of eating, he frequently took emetics. When he was proclaimed emperor, his mother reportedly gave him up for dead. This is perhaps why one of his few edicts in his brief tenure as emperor was to ban astrologers from Rome.

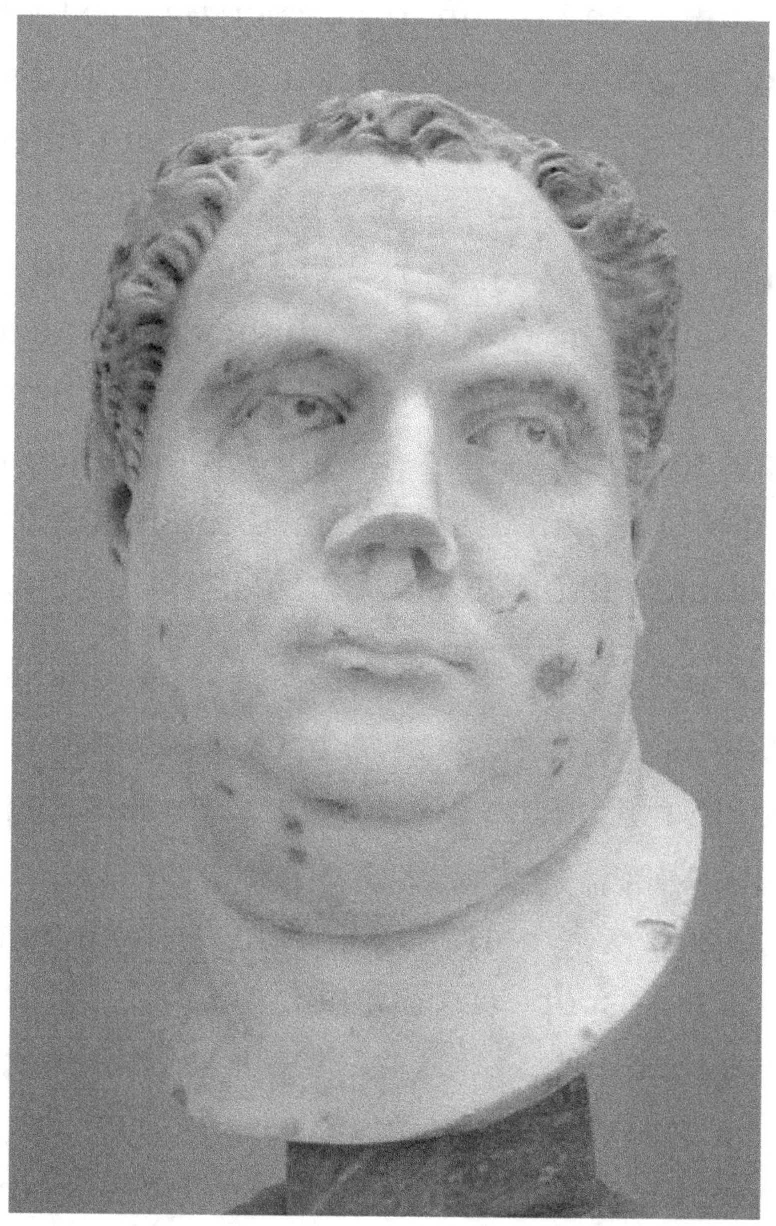

A bust of Vitellius

Many were surprised that Galba assigned him the important post of general in Lower Germany, a rich province with many troops, but perhaps Galba thought that such an obese man who was constantly in debt would be no threat. Otho made no move to remove him, and that proved to be his undoing. Vitellius proved popular with the troops, as he was apparently a friendly man with the common touch. He was equally happy eating with mule drivers as he was with consuls. He seemed not to mind who his company was, at least as long as he was eating.

There might have been more than a bit of guile in this, because the troops soon proclaimed him emperor. Galba had been assassinated, and he quickly marched on Otho. This occurred despite the bad omen of his recently built equestrian statues breaking at the legs. They had been poorly made, but later, after his rule had ended, people said he could not support the heavy weight of the office.

Once he arrived in Rome and became emperor in fact as well as in name, his eating knew no bounds. Vast sums of the treasury were spent on lavish feasts. One dish he had designed was called "Shield of Minerva, Defender of the City," which Suetonius described: "In this he mingled the livers of pike, the brains of pheasants and peacocks, the tongues of flamingoes and the milt of lampreys, brought by his captains and triremes from the whole empire, from Parthia to the Spanish strait."

His fiscal policy was as bad as his diet. Having been in debt most of his life, he now took revenge on the money lenders and tax collectors, putting many to death. He also executed anyone who spoke poorly of him, especially comedians and astrologers. On the other hand, he gave sumptuous gifts to everyone else, emptying the state coffers just like he had emptied his own.

Ultimately, nothing could not save him. Rebellion once again broke out in the provinces, and Vespasian marched on Rome. Vitellius's soldiers and servants abandoned him, and he was found hiding in the abandoned lodge of his door-keeper. Suetonius explained what happened when Vespasian's soldiers found him: "He did not cease to beg that he be confined for a time, even in the prison, alleging that he had something to say of importance to the safety of Vespasian. But they bound his arms behind his back, put a noose about his neck, and dragged him with rent garments and half-naked to the Forum. All along the Sacred Way he was greeted with mockery and abuse, his head held back by the hair, as is common with criminals, and even the point of a sword placed under his chin, so that he could not look down but must let his face be seen. Some pelted him with dung and ordure, others called him incendiary and glutton, and some of the mob even taunted him with his bodily defects. He was in fact abnormally tall, with a face usually flushed from hard drinking, a huge belly, and one thigh crippled from being struck once upon a time by a four-horse chariot, when he was in attendance on Gaius as he was driving. At last on the Stairs of Wailing, he was tortured for a long time and then dispatched and dragged off with a hook to the Tiber."

Now Vespasian was in charge, and the entire empire would soon breathe a sigh of relief to find itself in capable hands. Like many emperors before him, various omens had signaled that he would rise to glory. Once when he was eating breakfast, a dog came in from the street carrying a human hand in its maw and dropped it under Vespasian's table. While this would put a modern man off his breakfast, it was considered a good omen, the hand being a symbol of rule. Another time when he was having dinner, an ox broke away from its plough and rushed inside to where he was eating. Everyone must have thought it would run rampant and kill everyone in the room, but instead the ox stopped in front of Vespasian and bowed its head as if showing humility and obedience to him.

Vespasian ruled for 10 years, showing himself to be a wise ruler. His two sons, who peacefully succeeded their father one after the other, were also good rulers. The chaos in the Roman Empire was, for a time, over.

Sadly, more trouble would come in following centuries. The year 193 would be the Year of the Five Emperors, while 238 would be the Year of the Six Emperors. The

Year of the Four Empires had shown that a man with the support of some legions had a chance at seizing power. Far too many would take that chance, and it helped lead to the ruin of one of the greatest empires the world has ever known.

Scandalous accounts of emperors did not end with Suetonius. In fact, the office seems to have gradually degraded over time. While there were good and even great emperors in the second, third, and fourth centuries, the number of bad emperors increased, and the average quality generally went down.

One who truly stands out is Elagabalus, who ruled from 218-222. Just 14 when he took the purple, he was brought into power by a coup and assassination of his predecessor, engineered by his mother and grandmother. He took on the name Marcus Aurelius Antoninus Augustus, but he has gone down in history as Elagabalus after the name of the Syrian sun god for whom he was a priest, having been born in Emesa (modern Homs).

Perhaps his greatest transgression was trying to meddle with Roman state religion, a highly conservative edifice of entrenched powers. Elagabalus put his Syrian deity as the head of the Roman pantheon, replacing Jupiter, which understandably outraged the priesthood and many of the common people. He also had a portrait of himself put above the altar of Victory in the Roman Senate. The senators were in the habit of making regular offerings to the altar, and now if they did so it looked like they were making offerings to the new emperor.

After hurting religious sensibilities, he undermined the economy by devaluing the currency and reducing the amount of silver in the coins.

Moral scandals soon followed religious and political ones. As the historian Cassius Dio related:

> "He married many women, and had intercourse with even more without any legal sanction; yet it was not that he had any need of them himself, but simply that he wanted to imitate their actions when he should lie with his lovers and wanted to get accomplices in his wantonness by associating with them indiscriminately. He used his body both for doing and allowing many strange things, which no one could endure to tell or hear of; but his most conspicuous acts, which it would be impossible to conceal, were the following. He would go to the taverns by night, wearing a wig, and there ply the trade of a female huckster. He frequented the notorious brothels, drove out the prostitutes, and played the prostitute himself. Finally, he set aside a room in the palace and

there committed his indecencies, always standing nude at the door of the room, as the harlots do, and shaking the curtain which hung from gold rings, while in a soft and melting voice he solicited the passers-by. There were, of course, men who had been specially instructed to play their part. For, as in other matters, so in this business, too, he had numerous agents who sought out those who could best please him by their foulness. He would collect money from his patrons and give himself airs over his gains; he would also dispute with his associates in this shameful occupation, claiming that he had more lovers than they and took in more money. This is the way, now, that he behaved alike toward all alike who had such relations with him; but he had, besides, one favourite 'husband,' whom he wished to appoint Caesar for that very reason. …

"…When trying someone in court he really had more or less the appearance of a man, but everywhere else he showed affectations in his actions and in the quality of his voice. For instance, he used to dance, not only in the orchestra, but also, in a way, even while walking, performing sacrifices, receiving salutations, or delivering a speech. And finally, — to go back now to the story which I began, — he was bestowed in marriage and was termed wife, mistress, and queen. He worked with wool, sometimes wore a hair-net, and painted his eyes, daubing them with white lead and alkanet. Once, indeed, he shaved his chin and held a festival to mark the event; but after that he had the hairs plucked out, so as to look more like a woman. And he often reclined while receiving the salutations of the senators. The husband of this 'woman' was Hierocles, a Carian slave, once the favourite of Gordius, from whom he had learned to drive a chariot."

Cassius Dio went on to write that Emperor Elagabalus would correct people who referred to him as "Lord," saying, "I am a lady." He also reported that the emperor asked many surgeons if they could remove his penis and make an incision to create a vagina. No surgeon would undertake this task for fear of killing the emperor, so Elagabalus remained physically male.

Finally, the Praetorian Guard had enough. Elagabalus and his mother were killed, stripped naked, beheaded, and had their bodies dragged through the streets of Rome. His successor, Severus Alexander (r. 222-235), erased his name from monuments and had Elagabalus's statues re-carved in his own image.

It is difficult to know the truth about Elagabalus's reign, because he had so deeply insulted Roman traditions that contemporary historians were willing to repeat any number of tales about him. Yet tales of his many eccentricities came from numerous sources. Whatever the truth about his personal life, this compulsive teenager was certainly a disruptive force.

The possibility that Elagabalus was gender fluid has been debated by historians for quite some time and brings up the role that such people had in Roman society. Intersex individuals are noted in many written and artistic sources. Numerous sculptures have been preserved that at first glance show a beautiful, well-proportioned woman, but at second glance reveal a penis, often an erect one. One statue in the Getty Museum in Malibu shows what from one angle appears to be a nude sleeping woman, but if the viewer moves to the other side they see this "woman" has a penis. Another statue housed in the Louvre is more explicit - a figure who looks otherwise female is lifting her skirts to reveal an erect penis. Wall paintings from Pompeii show randy satyrs running after intersex people, apparently unaware that they are not "true" women.

In the Roman Republic, intersex individuals were viewed with fear and disgust. The Romans had no knowledge of genetics or how such an individual could naturally be born, so they assumed that they were the work of the gods, a warning of moral corruption. Romans were fascinated with strange births and deformities, and since they were keen on determining the future based on animal sacrifices, they naturally applied this to humans born different. In fact, since intersex individuals were considered ill omens, they were usually killed at birth. This was done with great ceremony, with 27 virgins singing hymns to Ceres and Persephone while the baby was placed in a box and drowned.

  Oddly, the gods were an exception to this loathing. Having their own rules, it was not considered wrong for a deity to show aspects of both sexes. The Romans coined the term hermaphrodite for intersex people, from the name of the ancient Greek god Hermaphroditus, the offspring of Hermes and Aphrodite. Like so many Greek deities, Hermaphroditus was incorporated into the Roman pantheon.

  The story of this strange deity started relatively normally. Born male, Hermaphroditus was raised by nymphs on Mount Ida in what is now Turkey. He grew into a beautiful youth and at the age of 15 went off to wander the world. While he was in Caria, on the west coast of Anatolia, he explored a wood and came across the nymph Salmacis bathing in a pool. Salmacis was taken by the youth's good looks but he refused her advances. Thus,

Hermaphroditus goes down in history as the only teenage boy to reject a nymph. After she left in a huff, Hermaphroditus bathed in the same pool.

What he didn't know was that Salmacis was sneaking up on him. Suddenly she jumped in the pool, wrapped herself around him, and asked the gods that they should never be separated. The gods listened and fused their natures into one. Hermaphroditus became, to all appearances, a female except for having a penis and testicles.

Hermaphroditus was horrified by his transformation and asked the gods to curse the pool so that if anyone bathed in it, they too would suffer the same fate. He went on to become a minor deity for both the Greek and Roman civilizations, worshipped by hermaphrodites and effeminate men.

By the 1st century CE, attitudes had changed toward intersex individuals. Loathing had given way to fascination, and intersex babies were no longer killed in religious ceremonies. It was then that the numerous artistic depictions of them were made.

The famous natural philosopher Pliny the Elder, writing in *Natural History*, noted:

> "Persons are also born of both sexes
> combined—what we call hermaphrodites,

formerly called *androgyni* and considered as portents, but now as entertainments. Pompey the Great among the decorations of his theatre placed images of celebrated marvels, made with special elaboration for the purpose by the talent of eminent artists; among them we read of Eutychis who at Tralles was carried to her funeral pyre by twenty children and who had given birth 30 times, and Alcippe who gave birth to an elephant—although it is true that the latter case ranks among portents, for one of the first occurrences of the Marsian War was that a maidservant gave birth to a snake, and also monstrous births of various kinds are recorded among the ominous things that happened. Claudius Caesar writes that a hippo-centaur was born in Thessaly and died the same day; and in his reign we actually saw one that was brought here for him from Egypt preserved in honey. One case is that of an infant at Saguntum which at once went back into the womb, in the year [218 BC] in which that city was destroyed by Hannibal.

"Transformation of females into males is not an idle story. We find in the Annals that in the consulship [171 BC] of Publius Licinius Crassus and Gaius Cassius Longinus a girl at Casinum was changed into a boy, under the observation of the parents, and at the order of the augurs was conveyed away to a desert island. Licinius Mucianus has recorded that he personally saw at Argos a man named Arescon who had been given the name of Arescusa and had actually married a husband, and then had grown a beard and developed masculine attributes and had taken a wife; and that he had also seen a boy with the same record at Smyrna. I myself saw in Africa a person who had turned into a male on the day of marriage to a husband; this was Lucius Constitius, a citizen of Thysdritum … (It is said that) at the birth of twins neither the mother nor more than one of the two children usually lives, but that if twins are born that are of different sex it is even more unusual for either to be saved; that females are born more quickly than males, just as they grow older more quickly; and that movement in the womb is more frequent in the case of males, and males are usually carried on the right side, females on the left."

Sex and Rome

Anyone who has read Roman histories or watched certain movies or television shows about Rome might think that the Romans were extremely lewd. There is no shortage of phallic and other sexual imagery, not only as graffiti but as high art and religious iconography. In Pompeii, archaeologists even uncovered a finely made marble statue of Pan copulating with a goat that once graced the garden of a wealthy villa. It seems the Romans were up for anything.

In reality, this was not the case. While they certainly had an earthier sense of humor, plus a more candid view of sex and the randiest gods of the ancient world, in practice, most Romans were fairly conservative about sexual matters. Women were expected to be virgins when they got married, and men had strict guidelines of behavior so they would not be considered effeminate.

In other words, men had to seem manly. They were not supposed to act in an overly refined manner, but rather to act gruff, honest, and direct. They were not supposed to pluck their eyebrows or use makeup or wear overly fine clothes or jewelry. They were supposed to prefer the company of other men and not spend too much time with or show too much affection for women.

This is not to say that they were supposed to enjoy the company of other men too much. While gay sex was common in the Roman world, a man was considered effeminate if he took the passive position. Thus, passive partners were in high demand. Men with a predilection for gay sex generally went for male prostitutes or slaves, whether of age or underage. This was generally not looked down upon as long as one remained the active partner. There was no word for homosexuality in Latin, and men who dallied with passive males were not considered different or unusual as long as they did their duty by getting married to a woman and starting a family.

Of course, there were homosexuals in Roman society, and there are even references to such men going through marriage ceremonies, although they were not recognized as valid by Roman law. There is little textual evidence for lesbian sex other than a few passing references and some love spells, but that is because the vast majority of texts were written by men. One can safely assume that it was as prevalent as in any other culture, albeit hidden behind closed doors and now all but lost to history.

For straight sex, one had to be careful. Female virginity was highly prized, because one wanted to be sure that any child born after the wedding was the groom's, or it could put the family wealth and inheritance in jeopardy. Thus, unmarried Romans indulged in all sorts of sexual practices that would leave the hymen intact and not risk pregnancy. This is still common today in cultures that value virgin brides.

For those who were a little more adventurous, or those married women who had had enough of childbearing, there was a natural birth control called *silphium*. This herb grew in North Africa and was a natural abortifacient. One would drink its juice to "purge the uterus." It proved so effective that it was in high demand, to the extent that it appears to have gone extinct by the middle of the 1st century CE. The reason for this was an intersection of factors that almost guaranteed that it would go extinct. First, it only grew in an area called Cyrene in what is now eastern Libya, on a thin strip of coastal slopes measuring about 125 miles (201km) by 35 miles (40km) that caught the Mediterranean rains. It also could not be transplanted. Its seeds would not bear a plant, and even trying to move an entire plant never worked.

Not only was it popular as an all-natural morning-after pill, but it tasted delicious and its pungent sap was used for a variety of products: It was turned into perfume, worked well as a preservative for other plants, and if fed to sheep it made their meat tender and flavorful. It could also be eaten, either raw or in recipes. One popular recipe involving *silphium* called for its sap to be dried and grated over braised flamingo.

Birth control wasn't its only medical use. *Silphium* was also rubbed into the bites of mad dogs and used to fumigate the rear end of someone suffering from growths on the anus.

With such a huge demand, it is not surprising that it was overharvested, even though the Romans put strict controls on this. With *silphium* selling at sky-high prices, literally worth its weight in silver, there was plenty of motive to harvest it illegally. Also, local shepherds grazed their flocks on *silphium* fields in order to improve the meat, despite there being strict punishments for doing so.

As supplies grew scarcer and scarcer, the government began to worry. Julius Caesar went so far as to keep 1,500 pounds of it in the treasury building, but it was a rearguard battle. 100 years later, the plant was apparently extinct. Modern botanists are trying to find it again, hoping that a few plants have survived, but their efforts are stymied by the ongoing fighting in Libya. The Romans mention a far inferior variety of *silphium* growing in northern Iran and Syria, but it isn't clear if this was the same plant or a close stand-in sold by hucksters. Either way, neither of those two regions are very hospitable to Western botanists at the moment, so botanists may never recover the *silphium*, seemingly consumed to extinction by the short-sighted ancients.

Interestingly, the seeds of the *silphium* are shaped like a heart, and some researchers believe that this is the reason people associate that shape with the anatomical heart (which isn't actually heart-shaped) and romance.

One unseemly aspect of Roman sexuality is that fact that much of it was non-consensual. Slaves of both sexes and all ages were considered fair game for the sexual advances of their owners, and they could do nothing to object short of running away or committing murder.

One notorious case of slave abuse was that of Hostius Quadra, who lived during the reign of Augustus. The stoic philosopher Seneca the Younger wrote of him, "There was one Hostius Quadra whose obscenity formed a model for everything that was lewd on the stage. He was rich and avaricious, a very slave to his millions. He was eventually murdered by his own slaves, but the late Emperor Augustus considered his murder undeserving of punishment, and as good as declared that he had been justly slain. This man's lust knew no distinction of sex. Among other things, he had mirrors constructed of the kind just mentioned, that reflected images of abnormal size, causing, for example, a finger to exceed the size of an arm in length and thickness. He so arranged his mirrors that he could see all his accomplices' movements, and could gloat over the imagined proportions of his own body."

Many of the slaves and prostitutes used by men were underage. Freeborn children, both girls and boys, were legally protected from sexual advances, and child molestation was a capital crime, but the enslaved enjoyed no such protection. There were a variety of terms for youthful, pubescent, and prepubescent boy slaves, and they were often discussed in the plays and poetry of the time. In a farce written around 30 BCE by Quintus Novius, the male youth is held up to be a better lover than a woman, so long as he remains relatively hairless. Some of these boys were known to be little more than toddlers, but their owners were more embarrassed by their poor manners about the house than their tender age.

There are numerous love poems and songs written by masters about their favorite boy slave. In fact, posterity has preserved as many poems to boys from the Roman world as to female lovers, and they show a remarkably similar tone of adoration, love, and jealousy. The poet Martial (c. 40–103 CE) saw a boy as superior to a wife, writing, "The sulks and pride of these boys and their petulant quarrels … I prefer to a dowry of a million sesterces." The poet Tibullus (c. 55-19 BCE) wrote numerous elegies to a youth named Marathus, and the poet falls into agonies of jealousy when he discovers Marathus is enamored with a girl. Marathus is not a Roman name, so scholars have assumed that he, too, was a slave.

Perhaps not surprisingly, the opinions of the slaves

themselves went unrecorded.

An Enduring Archaeological Mystery

One object has been the subject of an archaeological mystery for decades. It is none other than the Roman dodecahedron, a hollow object with 12 flat pentagonal faces, each with a hole. The holes are usually of varying sizes, and each corner of the polygon tends to have a little knob. They are made of bronze or sometimes stone. The interior is hollow. Sometimes they are engraved with decorative grooves around the holes. The entire object ranges from 4-11 centimeters wide.

A picture of Roman dodecahedrons

The term dodecahedron is a purely descriptive name because researchers have no idea what the Romans called them. To date, there is no written or visual record of them at all, and thus speculation as to their use is rife. A little more than 100 of them have been found, mostly in Germany and France, but as far east as Hungary and as far north as Wales. They seem to date from the second and third centuries CE, although the context in which many were found is unclear, so this dating is uncertain. Several were found in coin hoards, indicating that they were valued. It seems significant that they were made during a relatively limited time period, appear to be rare, and come from a limited geographic area. They are all in northern areas of the empire. None have been found in the southern or eastern reaches of the Roman Empire.

One explanation is that they are candle holders since two of them have been found with traces of wax inside, but wax was used for a variety of things other than candles, and they are oddly shaped for a candle holder. Having holes on each face, generally of varying sizes, might be good for holding candles of varying sizes, but it also allows wax to drip through the dodecahedrons onto whatever surface it is sitting on.

Another prosaic explanation is that they are frameworks for knitting, like the modern knitting Nancy. The idea is that the yarn was wound around the little knobs on the corners, the holes being so it could be held at any angle. By winding the yarn around the dodecahedron in certain ways, it could be used to make various knitted objects. Perhaps most were made of wood and have since vanished, with only the more elegant ones having survived. Supporters of this theory point out that the dodecahedrons are found only in northern parts of the empire where knitted goods would be needed.

Several modern experimenters have used reproductions of Roman dodecahedrons to knit various objects, but this theory has a couple of problems. Most importantly, there is no evidence supporting the existence of the knitting Nancy prior to about 400 years ago. Moreover, it begs the question of why such a mundane object would be laboriously made out of stone or bronze and be considered valuable enough to be hidden in a hoard. Finally, the smallest examples measure only four centimeters across, hardly sufficient for comfortable knitting.

Other explanations include that they were dice for gambling, with the size of the holes representing different values, or religious or magical objects. The latter is more a sign of helplessness than an actual explanation, as archaeologists tend to use the "ritual object" interpretation whenever they can't figure out what something is.

Yet another explanation is that they were used as a

standard measuring tool, perhaps for pipes, with the variously sized holes acting as measurements. This idea, however, seems to fail based on the fact that the dodecahedrons come in differing sizes and do not have any sort of standardization.

A more intriguing explanation is that they were range finders. Given that one can hold up a dodecahedron and look through a smaller and a larger hole, one can use mathematics to determine the range of an object viewed through the holes, assuming one knows the height of the object being observed. This is done by holding the dodecahedron up to the eye with the smaller hole closer to the eye and looking through the large hole opposite. If the dodecahedron is too close to the eye, the user sees both holes. If it is too far, the user sees only the nearest hole. The distance between the device and the eye can be adjusted, no doubt on some sort of stable platform with a measuring rod to get to a distance where he or she can see the circumferences of the two holes as perfectly superimposed. This is a specific angle of view that can then be used for measurements. Knowing the angle of view and a bit of quick math involving the known height of the object will give its distance. This certainly would have been useful for firing ballistae (Roman artillery that shot large arrows) at fortifications.

The problem with this theory is that there are many

visual depictions of Roman siege techniques, plus numerous written descriptions of battles, and there is no image or description of a dodecahedron. It also begs the question of why they were only found in northern areas and generally away from Rome's borders, where one would think they would have been of greater use. Although it could perhaps have been used for some sort of peaceful engineering works, there are many visual and written sources for those too, and they do not mention the dodecahedron. There is also the lack of any sort of measuring platform on which to put the device.

Another theory is that they were used in a similar fashion explained above to gauge the spring and autumnal equinox. This was especially important in northern areas in order to plant winter grain in order to optimize productivity. The dodecahedron would be placed on a horizontal plate on a sunny day, and around noon, the user would measure the light falling through two openings opposite each other against a ruler set on the horizontal plate. This would give the angle of the sun at noon for that day, thereby giving the date.

However, this theory is again undermined by a complete lack of mention of the device in the rich visual and textual evidence that exists for Roman astronomy and agriculture, two sciences that were especially preserved by later cultures. There is also a lack of the supposed support plate with measurement markings that would be an essential part of any such system. It also ignores the fact that ancient societies had been able to determine the equinox with proficient accuracy as far back as the Neolithic Period. The Romans, like many civilizations before them, already had a very accurate calendar.

As this all suggests, no theory about the Roman dodecahedron lacks major problems. It appears that until historians come across a pictorial representation of one or uncovers an inscription explaining their use, the mystery of these bizarre objects will continue to fuel speculation, like so much else about the ancient Romans.

Online Resources

Other mysterious titles by Charles River Editors

Other books about Rome by Charles River Editors

Other books about ancient history by Charles River Editors

Other books about Rome on Amazon

Further Reading

Beard, Mary et al. *Religions of Rome: A Sourcebook, Vols. 1 & 2.* Cambridge, United Kingdom: Cambridge University Press: 1998.

Cassius Dio. *Roman History.* Loeb Classical Library.

Harvard, CT: Harvard University Press, 1927.

Guhl, E. and W. Koner. *The Romans: Their Life and Customs*. London United Kingdom: Senate, 1994.

Hubbard, Thomas K., editor. *Homosexuality in Greece and Rome: A Sourcebook of Basic Documents*. Oakland, CA: University of California Press, 2003.

Jones, Prudence and Nigel Pennick. *A History of Pagan Europe*. New York City, New York: Routledge, 1995.

MacMullen, Ramsay. *Paganism in the Roman Empire*. New Haven, CT: Yale University Press, 1981.

Owen, Tomas, trans. *Geōponika: Agricultural Pursuits*. London, United Kingdom: 1806.

Pliny the Elder. *Natural History*. Bohn's Classical Library. London, United Kingdom: George Bell & Sons, 1900.

Sinnigan, William G., and E. R. Boak. *A History of Rome to A.D. 565, Sixth Edition*. New York City, New York: MacMillan Publishing Company, Inc. 1977.

Sparavigna, Amelia Carolina. "Roman Dodecahedron as dioptron: analysis of freely available data," in *arXiv*, 2012. https://arxiv.org/ftp/arxiv/papers/1206/1206.0946.pdf Retrieved 3/28/20.

Sparavigna, Amelia Carolina. "A Roman Dodecahedron for measuring distance," in *arXiv*, 2012. https://arxiv.org/ftp/arxiv/papers/1204/1204.6497.pdf Retrieved 3/28/20.

Suetonius. *The Twelve Caesars*. Loeb Classical Library. Harvard, CT: Harvard University Press, 1914.

Wagemans G.M.C., "The Roman Pentagon Dodecahedron, An Astronomic Measuring Instrument for Determining the optimal sowing date for winter grain." https://www.romandodecahedron.com/the-hypothesis Retrieved 3/30/20.

Free Books by Charles River Editors

Discounted Books by Charles River Editors

We have titles at a discount price of just 99 cents everyday. To see which of our titles are currently 99 cents, click on this link.